"But God is Faithful;
He will not suffer you to be tempted
beyond that which ye are able to bear"

Faithful is HE

Birdie L. Houston

©copyright 2018 Birdie L. Houston

Not Just Alphabets Publishing

Las Vegas, Nevada

All Not Just Alphabets Publishing titles, AJ Houston, wordart, imprints and lines distributed are available at special quantity discounts for bulk purchases for sales promotion, fund raising, premiums, educational, institutional and library use.

Copyright © 2018 by Birdie L. Houston. All rights reserved.

No part of this work may be reproduced or transmitted in any form or by any means, electronic or mechanical, including photocopying and recording, or by any information storage retrieval system without the prior written permission of A.J. Houston or Not Just Alphabets. Email notjustalphabets@gmail.com address to Permissions.

Printed in the U. S. A.

Library of Congress Catalog Card Number:

ISBN: 978-1-7338810-3-6

Dedication

This book is dedicated to the memory of my mother, Quintella Mary Perry Smith, and my father, Albert Austin, without whom I would not be here. In spite of the obstacles put before me, they did bring me into the world and nurture me until I was able to take care of myself So, thanks, Mama and Daddy for my life.

I want to also add a dedication to the memory of our two children who have passed on before us. They are Tonia Yvette Houston, born April 6, 1957 and died September 1958 and Regina Kim Houston. Regina was born August 1959 and died November, 1959. J.J. and I loved you both so much, but God knew best. Thanks to God for the time we did have our two lovely girls with us.

-Birdie L. Houston-

Jimmie Jay Houston I
and
Birdie Lee Austin - Houston

Together for More Than 45 Years

Special Dedication

This special dedication to my close friends Oretha Johnson, and her daughter, Beverly Smith and her husband, Wade. We met back in 1963, and watched each other's children grow up. Beverly's children Regina and Wende are our God children, and we love them very much. Oretha and I have been through some great times in the Lord and some trying times with our husbands, R. T. and Jimmie Jay, who were childhood friends. The death of R.T. many years ago was very hard on us all. We remain friends and fellow Christians, sharing the love of God with whomever we can, and encouraging one another in the love of our Lord and Savior, Jesus Christ.

-Thank you Always -
Birdie

Faithful is HE

Chapter I

Faithful is HE

My first recollection of life came when I was very small, maybe 4 or 5 years old. I was calling for one of the many ladies who were in this house (I don't remember whose house) and letting her know that her "trick" had arrived. I found out later that it was a whore house and my mother, Quintella Mary Anderson, was one of "the ladies of the night." The place was Wink, Texas in the early thirties. This was a small town in far West Texas.

My mother had only a third-grade education. She had her first child when she was 13 years old, my brother, Wardell. My mother told me that when she was 13, years old, her mother (who was separated from her father) told her to go to another town in Arkansas to nurse her father while he was ill. At this time, she and her mother, along with several other families, lived in a camp in Noblelake, Arkansas, where they worked and lived together. A young man who lived in the camp that mama knew, overheard the conversation. Evidently, he had his eye on Mama all the time, so when mama left for the bus station, the young man stopped her and talked her into making a trip all right, but not to the town where her daddy was. Mama said she and the young man went to another town and holed up for a week. They had a "grand" time together and her poor father was left all alone.

When her mother found out that Mary (as mother was called) didn't make it to where she was supposed to go, it was too late. Mother was already pregnant with Wardell. She could not go to school pregnant, so she had a big problem. She had to give him up for adoption because in those days, pregnancy before marriage was a real disgrace. Her father put her out of his house and she had to find a way to survive. What an awful thing to happen to a 13-year-old girl back in the early 1900's! (My mom was born in 1906). Wardell was adopted by a family by name of Johnson. The family had money and owned a lot property and houses. This was quite unusual for Blacks in those days. Wardell had several step sisters and brothers. Sometime after he was adopted, the Johnson family moved to Chicago, Illinois, where they acquired a lot of property. When Mrs. Johnson died, she left quite a bit of money and property to Wardell. His step 'brothers and sisters were very jealous of him because of it. He refused to live in any of the houses he owned. Instead, he lived in the men's YMCA on Madison Avenue in Chicago.

Wardell was afraid that if he lived in any home that his mother had willed him, his step brothers or sisters might kill him. He chose not to have much to do with them after his mother's death. After Wardell's death in Chicago several years ago, my sister Erma Jean and I went there to take care of his affairs. We met some of his step family members. We could readily see why Wardell chose to ignore their repeated requests to join them for a meal or a get together. They displayed very selfish and greedy attitudes while we were there. I was glad when we left Chicago. We have not seen or heard from them since that time.

Faithful is HE

We also had another sister named Mary Belle. She is 10 years older than I am. Mother left her in Arkansas with her mother. Mary came to Wink to be with us when she was about 25 years old. She brought her only child, Georgia Mae, with her when she came to Wink. Georgia was about 3 or 4 years old then. You will be introduced to the other children later in the book. I believe mom was in her early twenties when she came to Wink, Texas. She came because there was an "oil boom." This means that oil was discovered in that area, and many men were needed to work the oil fields. The money was good for that time, of course, the "ladies of the night" swarmed in to capitalized on the "quick money." Mom told me once that she only planned to stay in Wink a short while, but she wound up over the years she lived in Wink, several children were born to her. First, I, Birdie, was born on August 1, 1932, Marvin on March 14, 1933; Joe on August 27, 1934, Erma Jean on February3, 1941 and Patricia Ann on March 17, 1944.

In our little town of Wink, Texas, most of the Black people live in what was called "Colored Town," as usual, across the railroad tracks. In our section, which consisted of one "main" street, and a few other short streets, our homes were called "shotgun houses." That meant that all the rooms were in one straight line with one common hallway. There was a doorway at the front of the house and at the first room, then the rest of the rooms were built in a line all the way back to the kitchen. There were no bathrooms. We had no indoor plumbing. We went to the bathroom in "outdoor toilets," which were usually located directly behind our houses. Each toilet consisted of a small room with a hole or two cut in wood and fashioned where we could sit over the hole. There was a door with an inside and outside latch. We could lock ourselves in while using it. Our toilet tissue was the "Sears" catalogue. Our Sears catalogue was multi-purpose. We all looked forward to receiving it, and both the grownups and children had use for it. Grownups would look at it and "wish" they could buy the items in the book. Hence, the name "wish book." We children would look at the pictures in the catalog and cut paper dolls from it to play with, and then we'd use it to finish our business in the toilet. We would rub the sheets together until they were soft. Then they were ready for use. That was our "Scott" tissue. I believe I was in college before I even knew toilet tissue existed.

We did have running water outside the house later on in our childhood, but before that, Mama bought water from the "water man." There was a Spanish man named Nick who came through about three times a week and sold us a barrel of water. It cost 50 cents a barrel. I have no idea where the water came from, but we used it to drink, cook and wash with. God took care of us, because we trusted Nick to give us good clean water. There was no telling where that water came from. After a time, we got a hydrant in our back yard with running water. We would take our pots, pans and tubs out to the hydrant to draw water for use in the house. We thought nothing of it because it was all we knew. Everyone was glad not to have to use water in a barrel.

Faithful is HE

It is so funny now to think of us having to heat our bath water in a rusty tea kettle on a wood stove and bathe in an old tin tub. Many times, we would all bathe in the same water. I remember my brother, Joe, telling Mama, "I don't want to bathe in Birdie Lee's water anymore," So Mama let him pour out my bath water and use fresh, heated water for his bath. Can you imagine kids bathing in each other's water this day and time? We kids just did as we were told and kept on going. In my early childhood, we would wash our clothing once a week outside. My brothers would build a fire under this huge, black wash pot, fill it up with water and we would wait for the water to boil. Mama would put our homemade lye soap* in the water. (we had no granulated soap or purex). (The first granulated detergent I remember was Oxydol).

We used a washboard or "rub board" to loosen the dirt from our clothing. The rub board is a wooden slab with steel ridges three fourths the length of the board. There is an opening near the top to place our bar soap. We would scrub the clothes vigorously for a few minutes, rub soap on them and scrub them again until the dirt was loose or gone. Next we would place our white clothes in the wash pot and allow them to boil. They would boil for about an hour, then we would rinse them twice in tubs of water. In one tub mama would pour some bluing. (A blue liquid sold in bottles used to whiten clothes.) Our clothes would be so white and pretty. We would then hang them on the clothes line to dry. There is no smell like the smell of clean, white clothes that have been washed in lye soap and are hung on a clothesline to dry in the sunshine. During this time, we had no electricity. Everyone in our neighborhood used kerosene Lamps. Those are the lamps that people use for decoration now, but they were all we had when I was a young girl. We would keep kerosene in cans in the kitchen, so when our lamps had used it all up, we could add more kerosene. We had to be really careful, because one false move with the kerosene could cause a fire. We also had to keep the glass chimneys clean, since the constant burning would blacken them with soot. We would then trim the burnt part of the wick, wash the soot from the chimney, and add kerosene to have a brighter light. We studied our lessons by lamplight and did everything that had to be done at night by lamplight.

I remember one time my older brother, Marvin, struck a match to try to find something in a closet in our house. He dropped the match in a pile of clothing and started a fire. Our house burned down, and we lost everything. I must have been about 11 or 12 years old. Of course, we had to get another house. Our homes were heated with wood heaters and our mothers cooked on wood stoves. These stoves were made of iron and had hollow insides, so we could put the cut wood inside. We would then pour a little kerosene on the" kindling" (small pieces of wood and other combustibles) to start the fire. You have never tasted food like the food my mama cooked on the old wood stove. She cooked biscuits that were 3 or 4 inches high. They would be brown on the top and bottom. and so fluffy inside that you could "sop" syrup and butter for a while. She also made what we called "hoe cakes." This was a type of fried bread similar to pancakes, but a little different. We could make a meal of hoe cakes and syrup with a little bacon grease poured into the syrup. Often that was our meal. We seldom had money to buy meat.

Mama made cakes that were higher than the cakes we make today. I don't know what the difference was. But it seems that they were wider and higher than ours. She made the best prune cake I have ever tasted. I doubt if anyone even thinks that prunes could be good in a cake these days and times. Anyway, Mama was a great cook. She even learned how to cook Italian food by working for Italians. She made great dishes like "polentas", meal cooked by pouring hot water on it and seasoning it, then adding a meat concoction made of beef, chopped vegetables and a thick tomato sauce. The meat and sauce were poured over the cooked seasoned meal. Talking about mouth-watering, yum, yum. She also made some of the best spaghetti ever. My mama had a lot of good qualities, even though her moral conduct was bad for raising children. She did try to keep us together regardless of the way our home life was. She worked hard to keep a roof over our heads and food on our table. I believe she stopped actually turning "tricks" by the time I was in school.

But some things she did that were beyond reasoning. I remember her telling me that when I was very young (2 or 3 years old.), she would allow her friends. to give me whiskey to drink. She said I could turn up a shot glass and empty it in a flash. Then they would laugh as I grew limp. When Mama told me this after I was grown up, I cried like a baby. Just to think that my own mother would allow people to give me whiskey for amusement. This could account for my total dislike for whiskey and other strong alcoholic drinks. I remembered that her formal education was limited, and maybe she just didn't know any better. God gave me the strength to forgive her. Let me tell you about my early years in elementary school. In those days we had what was called a "one room" school house. That means there were grades one through seven in the same room. The teacher would call for them like so: 2nd grade mathematics, 4th grade reading, 5th grade English, etc., until all the grades had been taught for the day.

My best teacher was Mrs. Lummie Mae Walker. That sister was a good teacher. She really gave us little black children a good foundation. She was from a little town in Texas called Powell, just outside of Corsicana. She was the kind of teacher that would give you the answer twice, but on the third time you got a lick in your hand with her long ruler. Suddenly your memory would become really good. I thought I was disadvantaged until I went away to school and found I knew a lot more than some of the kids who went to the big, prestigious high schools. My friend, Eddie Robinson from Fort Worth, said the same thing. He reminded me that we learned so well under Mrs. Walker that if you woke us up from a sound sleep and asked certain questions about rules for doing math and other important things, we would be able to answer them without thinking. Those things stay with you for a lifetime. Eddie's sister, Bennie Mae and I were good friends from little girls, also Eddie's brother James was a friend. We were all products of Wink's little Black elementary School. During the time we were growing up, the teachers lived in the neighborhood, went to church with the students and knew all the parents. If we got in trouble and got a spanking at school, you can rest assured we would also catch it at home. It never came up that we might be psychologically messed up. In fact, our opinion did not count. If an adult said you did it, you got a whipping from the adult, and mama, too.

      The concept of "it takes a village to raise a child," was in full force when I came up. Most adults were concerned about us as kids and we didn't turn out too bad. They would take the responsibility to discipline us or show us the right way and nothing was said about it, but "thank you." Wouldn't our kids be different if things were like they used to be? Because my mother was not married and we all had different fathers, some people looked at us as trash. Those people did not want their children to play with us. We were often dirty and unkempt because we just didn't know how to keep ourselves clean. I guess this might explain why I always wanted my children to be clean and have combed hair even while lounging around the house or playing outside. I couldn't bear to see my girls with their hair sticking out on the top of their heads or wearing dirty shorts and tee shirts. It most assuredly explains why I was determined that all my children would have the same father. Imagine the embarrassment of telling your siblings' names and everyone having a different last name. Some of the mean-spirited people in our town would say of me, "I'll bet she'll have five children by the time she is 16." She's going to be just like her mother." But God was so faithful and gave me a firm resolve that what they said about me would not come true.

Chapter II

Faithful is HE

Maybe another reason people looked down on us was because Mama made "home brew" at home and sold it at home, also. We kids would help make it, wash beer bottles, fill and cap them. Then people would flock to our house and buy the home-made beer. I know we seldom had a full-time pastor. Mostly, we would have a preacher that would come to us on say 1st and 3rd Sundays and go to some other church on 2nd and 4th Sundays. My teacher, Mrs. Lummie Walker played the piano for the church. I longed to learn how to play the piano by just watching her. There was one preacher that used to hold us little girls on his lap and fondle us. At the time, I didn't realize what was going on, but as I recall incidents in my early life, I remember him patting us and rubbing us. This man seemed so religious that I doubt if any parent would have believed us, if we had told what he did. For the life of me, I can't remember his name.

I always worked hard, even as a young person of ten or twelve. My first job was for a Jewish family who owned the only "dry goods" store in Wink. That was the kind of store that sold clothing and housewares. I earned $3.00 per week. I had to clean their house each day after school. Evidently, I did a good job because I worked there a long time. Later on, I worked for an Italian family cleaning house. My salary was $6.00 per week. In those days $6.00 would buy a lot of groceries and clothes. You could get a stick of butter for a nickel, a loaf of bread for a dime, a bottle of RC for a nickel, a large Baby Ruth candy bar for a nickel, a pair of shoes for $1.95, etc... So, you see, six dollars would help a large family a great deal. I remember mama sending me to the store to buy a quarters worth of ground meat and a quarters worth of sausage mixed. Mama would make meat balls with gravy and bake those big, fluffy biscuits. We would all have plenty and have some left over.

Being the oldest child at home, I had the greater responsibility. I had to basically watch my brothers and sisters while my mother worked. I was only a few years older than the boys, so you can imagine what happened in our house when mama was gone. Fights!! Arguments!! About who was the boss. Mama made me learn how to transact business when I was about 12 years old. We were on welfare and I would go to the office and complete the necessary papers. We would get food like peanut butter, cheese, meats, butter, fruit, and clothing which was made by the poor women in what they called the "Sewing Room." This was a part of the New Deal that President Roosevelt began. It was his way of helping the poor people.

The women worked in the Sewing Room to sew clothing for their own children out of flower sack material. These clothes were then given out through the Welfare Program. In those days flour sack material was very colorful and sturdy. It made up beautifully into dresses for girls and shirts for boys. The men worked on construction gangs by building schools and other government buildings and receiving wages for it. The young men went to what was called the CCC Camps. That meant Civilian Conservation Corporation. In these camps they gave them work and training to keep them out of trouble and paid them a wage. We called it being "On Relief". In addition to taking care of her welfare business, mama would send me to the store to buy shoes for the other children, groceries for the family and whatever else needed to be done in the way of business. I didn't know I was too young to do this until I grew up and realized that most people don't send their 12-year-old children to take care of their business. I guess I was all she had to handle things. She would tell me exactly what to say and do. I would follow her instructions to the letter.

This was during the time when shoes, sugar and some other important things were "rationed." What that means is, we were at war (World War II) and certain goods were scarce. The government issued books of ration stamps which allowed you to buy these scarce things. The rationing limited the amount you could buy, so as to allow everyone access to the rationed items. After you used up your ration books, you had to wait a certain length of time before you would be issued another one. Once I was sent to buy myself some shoes in winter. I knew what kind of shoes my mom wanted me to buy, but I saw these white sandals that I fell in love with. I bought them, took them home, and mom was so mad, because we could not get more stamps till a good while in the future. I had to wear the sandals in the cold, snowy weather. At the age of about nine or ten I was exposed to the Gospel of Jesus Christ through a White lady named Mrs. Jarman. She came to Wink, Texas, all the way from Odessa, Texas, periodically. (Odessa is 60 miles from Wink in West Texas.) Being that young, I don't remember whether it was weekly or monthly, but I do remember it being regular.

She gave us incentives to learn Bible verses and we ate it up. She would encourage us to learn, the Blood verses, the Bread or Water verses and give prizes for those who memorized the verses assigned. She had a unique way of teaching that made us little Black children really want to learn. She also led us to Christ, I never forgot the experience even though I didn't quite understand the full implication of being "Born Again." I truly believe that experience was the only thing that saw me through those difficult years ahead. By writing this book, I wanted to show how, after my salvation, the Lord protected me until I was able to get nurturing in the Word in order to grow. "God is still faithful." I had a chance to meet Mrs. Jarman several years ago to let her know that through her ministry to us in Wink, I came to know the Lord as my personal Savior. She was in her 70's at the time. She was so glad to see me and hear about my life in Jesus. My friend, Jimmie Lou, who lives in Odessa, Texas, took me to see Mrs. Jarman.

I am ever so grateful to Jimmie Lou for allowing me to stay with her when my mother was ill in a hospital in Odessa. Jimmie let me spend the nights in her home and go to the hospital in the day time. Love you, Jimmie and Samuel. I know there are some who might say that what I went through wasn't as bad as what some people have experienced, but, when it is happening to you, it is just as bad as some other people's worst experiences. We can only give account of the things that happened to us. As I told you at the beginning, my mother was a very promiscuous woman. She would have sex with whomever. However, she would always have a man who lived in our home with us. This is primarily the reason people looked down on us and talked about us. The first man I remember was my brother, Marvin's father, whose name was W. Jones. He was a very dark, jealous man. He would leave our house and sweep the front yard with a broom, so he could tell if another man came while he was gone. If someone came, their tracks would be in the yard. We had no grass or trees in West Texas, only sand. He would fight mother and we were all very scared of him.

My brother Joe's father came next, Mr. Williams. He was also a gangster type. I believe he was a gambler. He would leave and stay gone for days at time. When he came back, he would have pockets full of money. He would give mama lots of money. I just barely remember when he left. I know I was glad when he did. The next one that I remember was Mr. Jimmy. He was a kind man who played the guitar and sang to us children. I really hated when he left. He seemed to really care about Marna and us more than any of the other men. You see, there was a pattern. A man would come to live with us for a while and then leave. After he left, mother would go to the hospital and "bring us back a baby." Pretty soon, another man would come to live with us, then leave, and presto, a new baby. I remember one of mama's friends told me "they are bringing your new baby from the hospital." So, I thought babies came from the hospital.

The man I most remember was Earnest Anderson Smith, the father of my baby sister, Patricia. He was a very educated man, but an abusive one. He fought mother and me, too. He wanted me to call him daddy. I would not because mother told me Albert Austin was my father. Besides, he was so mean to all of us. I did not want to call such an abusive man, daddy. Because I refused, he hit me. It was frightening. It's amazing how children love their parents unconditionally. At that time, Albert was doing nothing at all for me, but because mother said he was my father, I loved him. I did not want anyone to say anything negative about him. Earnest would be fine until he started drinking. He would get drunk, beat up my mother, have her face all swollen and eyes all black, then he would run us all out of our house down the street. The neighbors would let us come in until he would get sober and back to normal. While he was drunk, he would walk up and down the one main street in "Colored Town," and curse mother for everything he could think of.

One day Earnest decided to try to seduce me. Mother was at work and there was nobody home but me and him. He started to talk real soft and soothing to me to try to get me thinking about sex I guess. Then he took out his penis, which was fully erected (I didn't know this then, I just knew I had never seen anything so big). He said things like "let me put it in. I will rub it with Vaseline and it won't hurt a bit. You will love it, I promise." I believe to my soul that God, in His sovereignty gave me the back bone to stick to my guns and say emphatically, "NO." No amount of coaxing gave me even the remotest desire to give in. Isn't our God wonderful? I walked away from him without giving in, thank you, Lord. If I had any respect at all for him, that ended it. I was afraid to tell my mother, because in my heart, I did not feel that she would believe me. So, God gave me a defense that never allowed him to get close to me again in that manner.

When my grandfather in California died, mother had to go because she was his only child. I am told that he was a well-to-do person. He had houses, land and money. When Earnest learned this, he married my mother before they went to California. I did not know all this until I was an adult. While mama was gone, my sister, Mary Belle, took care of us. We had a hard time with her. She had us four, along with her daughter, our niece, Georgia Mae. We didn't have much to eat and she fussed at us all the time. I guess taking care of five children, instead of just one, was hard for a young woman of about 25 years old. After several months, mother came back from California without Earnest. It was an answer to my prayer. Every night I prayed that he would not come back with her. Our lives were pure hell while he lived with us. So, even at my young age, I knew that God answered prayer. I learned later in life that he had enticed mother to sign over much of her property to him, and he stayed behind to take advantage of it. We never saw him again.

Little Buster came to live with us after Mama came back from California. He was younger than Mama and loved to drink whiskey, party and fight. Mama would drink with him and they would fight on the weekends. Once Little Buster was fighting Mama and she stabbed him with an ice pick. The sheriff came and got Mama to put her in jail, but she had so many children at home, he made her promise to leave Little Buster alone or he would throw her in jail. Needless to say, she left him alone. There is one person who was in our lives that was like a real father to me. His name was Machell Franklin. He was one of the kindest men I have ever known. He and his wife, Elnora, would buy us shoes, clothes, toys or whatever we needed.

My father, Albert did nothing for me; neither did any of the men my mother let live with us. Machell was our next-door neighbor. He must have been sent by God. He was the one who would taste my bad cooking and tell me how good it was. He would smile and my self-esteem would go up. I will never forget what Machell and Elnora did to help us grow up in a difficult situation. They would buy shoes and clothes for us when we needed them and presents on holidays. They were not any kin to us, but just had compassion on a bunch of illegitimate kids. I learned that Machell died several years ago from natural causes and Elenora was killed by another woman in a gambling dispute. I was always singing then. It was kind of my outlet. In those days we only had the country western music and ballads like the big bands played--Duke Ellington, Tommy Dorsey, Jimmy Dorsey, and Jimmy Lunsford. We could buy books at the drug store with the lyrics to all the popular songs. I would buy the books and learn the lyrics and sing at home in the streets, etc... I loved singing and Machell would tell me I sounded good. He was the one positive role model in my life. It's amazing how God used what was available to carry me along until I could get some real Scriptural nurturing. When I was about 14, I started working, along with my mother, in the home of Mr. and Mrs. Lane Newbert, a middle aged white couple who had an insurance business in Wink. They had their business in the front and lived in the back of the building for many years before they built a beautiful brick home near where they had their business. I had to do basic house cleaning, washing and ironing clothes for the family of three. One thing I loved about Mrs. Newbert was that she always gave me and mama clothes and jewelry.

She was a very soft-spoken woman and was kind to my mother and me. We never had to work very hard at her home, and she would encourage us to sit at the lunch table and eat with her. In those days, that was not done. Needless to say, my mother and I loved working for the Newbert family. They had a daughter named Susie. Susie was in either grade school or junior high when I began working. She was very liberal in her thinking. She treated me like somebody. She liked to talk to me about things that were going on in her life. And I enjoyed it, too. Here was a young white girl that treated me like I was no different than she. So, going to work at Mrs. Newberts was almost like a holiday. I never shall forget their kindnesses to my family. We had nothing, but Mrs. Newbert gave so much to help us get through those early, hard years. My mother worked for Mrs. Newbert for many years until she was unable to work (she was in her seventies.) She didn't do very much work. Mrs. Newbert would pick mom up in her big Cadillac and bring her back home in about three hours. Everybody liked to watch that big fine Cadillac bring morn home. Mom would brag about it. That was a big thing to her to be picked up and brought home by Mrs. Newbert in her fine car. Mrs. Newbert would also pay Mama every week whether she worked or not. So, Mama was able to save her Social Security money. Everything was so cheap in Wink that she could live on the money Mrs. Newbert paid her. (All this was after her children grew up and left Wink.) I sincerely wish Mr. & Mrs. Newbert were alive so I could personally thank them for making our difficult life a little better. So, I will say thank you, to Susie their daughter, for her part in my growing up.

I was fifteen when I began to work part time for Barbara Jones, the music teacher for Wink High School. I would clean, wash, iron and baby sit in exchange for music lessons. Mrs. Jones bought my music and gave me singing and piano lessons. I loved working for Mrs. Jones. She was a very nice person, and she worked me hard in my music. I learned how to read music and play piano. This went on for about two years. By the time I was in the 11th grade, I knew a little bit more about piano and singing. Mother and I both worked a while for Mrs. Moore who owned a boarding house. In those days, she (Mrs. Moore) would fix breakfast, lunch and dinner for working people who had no time to cook for themselves. Mrs. Moore would cook big meals and serve them in the large dining room in her home. Mama and I would wash the dishes for her. She would give us the leftover food daily. Boy did we eat good when we brought food home from Mrs. Moore's. God truly blessed our big family through me and Mama working.

There was no school for Black children in the 11th and 12th grade, so I had to be sent away from home to boarding school to complete my high school work. I guess I was about 17 years old when I left home. I was sent to Mary Allen College Preparatory School in Crockett, Texas. This was a high school branch on the Mary Allen College campus. It was hard being away from home at 17. Especially, never having been away before, and here I was living in a college dormitory. I was homesick the first few months, but after that, I started to come around. Meeting new friends and having new experiences was like a shot in the arm. I learned well, made good grades and got used to being away from home. Isn't it amazing how God gives us the power to adapt to whatever conditions we encounter? Faithful is He.

Mary Allen College made an impact on my life that will remain forever. It was a Baptist School, and Dr. Green L. Prince was the president. He was one of the best Bible teachers of that time. He had around him, several great Bible teachers. They taught academics as well as Bible. We had Chapel every day. At the time, I rebelled against chapel and all that Bible teaching, but isn't it remarkable how God can reach us even when we don't realize it? We would hide in our rooms under the bed, in the closet, in the showers or wherever we thought we wouldn't be discovered, to keep from going to chapel. But our teachers and deans mostly always found us and marched us into chapel. Every now and then someone would outsmart them. That was very seldom, however.

I remember reading comic books and any other kind of book during chapel, but somehow the teaching still reached my heart. Dr. Prince taught us from the Revelations. He talked about the Seven Churches and the Candlesticks. That was my first-time hearing about them. He knew most of us by name, if he saw us not paying attention, he would call our names and embarrass us. When God said in Isaiah 55: 11,"My word shall not return unto me void," He meant that. I thought I was not paying attention, but I found the Word of God stuck with me until I was able to decipher what had happened. After high school, I stayed on at Mary Allen and went to college. I lived in the dormitory.

We would go home on Christmas and at the end of the school year. It was a long bus ride from Crockett to Monahans, Texas .. That's as far as that bus would take me. Then I had to take another bus to Wink. Life at Mary Allen College shaped my being in a positive way. I was learning about Jesus and the Christian life as well as, growing academically. I met people that have remained in my life through the years. Much of my character was shaped by the teachers and preachers that worked there. Two of my good friends would help me get on the right bus. They were Eli and Earlie Davis, who are here in Dallas. As

I write this text, I still have contact with many of my fellow students through the Mary Allen College Alumni Association - Dallas Chapter. They include: My play mother, Adelle Perry, Betty Jones, Eli and Earlie Davis, Roscoe and Doris Middleton, Fay Dean Crowder, Rubye Stewart, Merfay Gray, Verna, Veal, Naomi Lede', Wilson Andrews, May Gray, Hattie Faye Allen, Losie Branch Walker, Olivia Vonner, Rev. A. Charles Bowie and his wife, Bennie of Cleveland, Ohio, Betty and Claude B. Buster from Atlanta, and so many others.

Chapter III

Faithful is HE

I mentioned in a previous paragraph about the long bus ride home. Well, it was during one of these trips home that I met my husband, Jimmie Jay Houston. It was the year I turned 19 years old. I was going home for the Christmas holidays. The bus that went to Monahans was the Los Angeles, California bus. We met in Dallas, Texas at the Continental Trailways bus station. I had to ride from Crockett to Dallas and wait for about four or five hours for the Los Angeles bus. A friend, and fellow student, named Betty Carlock lived in Dallas, so she took me home with her until time for the bus to take me home. When Betty and I got off the bus, there was a small, medium brown skin young man in fatigues watching me out of the corner of his eye. At first, I ignored him, but then it became impossible, because he was looking at me openly by this time. I blushed, being embarrassed by his brazen looks. We walked on by him and went to Betty's house.

When we returned later that day, there he was looking me over from head to toe. I was offended and he knew it, but it didn't seem to bother him at all. Finally, it came time to board our bus. He walked up to me and took my arm, my overnight bag, and helped me up the steps. He asked if he could sit by me. I told him, "It's a free bus, sit wherever you want to." He did sit beside me and began to talk. Now that I'm older and wiser, I know I was no match for him. Here I was a sheltered girl of 19, who had never really had a date, from a town of 1,500 people and no experience with men, matching wits with this worldly, young marine. "Ha Ha! I was doomed from the start. Needless to say, he poured on the charm, told me many lies, which I swallowed hook, line and sinker. By the time we got to Monahans, I had kissed him and basically fallen for him. I gave him my right address, which is the first time I ever did that. I had met other service men on the way home over the course of a few years, but I always gave them the wrong name and address when they asked.

Jimmy Houston had a sister in Crockett, Texas, I found out later. She was married to one of the sweetest men I have ever met named Charles Freeman. He loved his Frankie and all his children, and all his kinfolks. (Our family included) He supported Frankie in whatever she did. They had four children. Jesselyn, Pamela, Rodney and Artie Mildred. They loved their cousins (our children), and often came to visit us or asked us to visit them. Jay, as we all called him, told Frankie he had a girl friend at Mary Allen College and he wanted her to take care of me. She came to the college to see me and we became good friends. She would visit me often, bring me nice dinners on Sundays and keep in touch all the time. She was always nice to me. Our bonding was one that lasted until she died in an automobile accident several years ago.

Jay wrote me many love letters and sent money to help me. I was not used to that, and I did not know how to receive it. He wrote letters that sounded like they came from the movies. I'll never forget a particular statement he made. It went like this, "What do you want, the moon? Just say the word and I'll take my lasso of love and bring it down for you." The boy was Baad! He told me later that he would write love letters for his friends and they would pay him, because he knew just how to express himself. Needless to say, I fell in love with this little impudent marine. Jay came from a big family, which I met later. I loved his mother, Mama Vinie. She treated me like I was her daughter. She even said I looked like her girls. He had seven siblings, three girls: Laverne, LaRena, and Edith; four boys: Charles Preston, (Jay was next), Charlie, Jr., Willie Ray, and Travis. Charlie, Jr. and I are the same age, and we had a lot in common. He was always really funny. He kept Jay and me laughing whenever we were around him. LaRena is the one Mama Vinie would send to Dallas to help me when our children were born. I will be forever grateful to Mama Vinie and Rena for that. Mama Vinie would tell Rena, "You go down to Dallas and keep those kids for Jay and Birdie. Make Birdie stay in bed six weeks. Don't let her sweep and pick up heavy things." What she said, she meant. Rena followed her instructions to the letter.

I really love his family. After Jay and I married, they were all that I had. They were my family, too. Our children grew up together, and we spent many, many Mother's days and Christmases in Greenville, Texas together. That was their home town and where Mama Vinie lived. We all shared lots and lots of happy holidays. Jay's sister, Laverne, and I had two of our children close together. We were good friends down through the years. I was very happy to be a part of their family. After Mama Vinie died, we stopped having our get-togethers and we have grown apart as a family. There was a shake-up at Mary

Allen College, which brought down its accreditation. It seems the registrar was selling transcripts and credits to older persons who had been teaching for years without official degrees. There were new laws passed requiring them to go to school further. They were afraid they couldn't pass, so this woman decided to "help" herself and them by doctoring transcripts and falsifying records, so they could keep their jobs. It is very difficult to keep these things hidden for long. So, somehow they got busted and the mess hit the fan. The State government came into the picture and confiscated records and transcripts of all students. They found out that we were being allowed to take overloads, I guess, for the money. But we who lived in the dormitory actually took the classes and bought the textbooks. We did not know what was going on until the State people came in. They stayed on campus for days, pulling records and questioning students and teachers.

Even though we were not a part of the conspiracy, we had to suffer with those who were; consequently, many hours were struck from our transcripts. I lost 30 hours for which I had bought books, taken the classes, and passed with good grades. This was a crushing blow and it was really discouraging to me. The registrar and some others got some prison time for being a part of the mess. I was a music education major in my senior year. At this time, I had already begun my student teaching at an elementary school in Crockett. In addition, my music teacher was getting me ready for my senior recital. Just think how awful it was to be told that you would not graduate after 4 years and 3 summers of going to college! I was crushed and did not know what to do at this point. I was disgusted with the situation and ripe for doing something crazy. In the meantime, I was being pressured by Jay to go all the way. I was really scared, because I knew what could happen. Here I was 21 years old and still not sexually active. All my friends talked about sex all the time. I had one experience when I was 15 years old, and it was the pits. I didn't know what all the fuss was about. I just know I did not enjoy sex. But I had a great love for Jay that could not be ignored.

I forgot to talk about my first love, Carroll Walker. He was about the best-looking man I had ever seen (I was 15 years). He was the usual kind of young black man, telling me if I did not go all the way with him, he could get someone else to. I wish I had known what I know now and said, "Be my guest." Anyway, I did go all the way with him just to "show my love." Oh, how I hate to admit this at this time. Young women are so deceived into believing they have to give in sexually to "show their love." In reality, love is not shown by giving in to sex. Gratification to the male species is the goal of that pack of lies. After sex is over, he is going on to his next conquest and many times we become just so many notches in his proverbial "belt." I wish I could give all young women a glimpse into the future, showing how they are going to feel when they grow up and think about the men who gave her this kind of ultimatum. By the way, my sexual experience with Carol was for the birds. I felt nothing and wondered what all the fuss was about. I felt violated and nasty after it was over. There is something about sin that makes your very person feel like you are covered with dung! Which is how I felt.

By the way, Carol married another woman while I was in college and had 10 children. Boy, am I glad we didn't get married! I heard he and his wife divorced and he died several years ago. I guess I must have slipped away from campus to go to the home of my friend Frankie, Jay's sister, who I told you about earlier. It's kind of hard to remember how I got there, but anyway, I did more than once. Jay and I would have our little trysts in their spare bedroom. After a few visits from Jay, I found that I was pregnant. I was a senior in college. By this time, I had somewhat recovered from the shake up by going to school an additional semester and completing all my courses except my student teaching and one course of French, which I was taking at the time. I was really scared about being pregnant. I remembered what the people in my home town used to say about me. They predicted I would have a houseful of kids before I was 16 years old, just like my mother. I was also frightened of my father. He had told Me if I ever got pregnant, he would kill me and I believed him. Albert Austin was not the kind of man who made idle threats. He was a man of his word, and I took him seriously.

I'm getting a little ahead of myself. I need to tell you about my job at the hospital. I got a job in the summer working at the Mary Allen College Hospital. I learned a lot of good things like how to do blood sugars, urine tests, and fill prescription, etc. In those days we could do that without being certified. I was trained by the Doctor. His name was Dr. James Hilliard. He was the first Black doctor I ever knew. He was a good doctor and a great help to the people of Crockett. When I discovered I was pregnant, I shared my problem with an older nurse who worked at the Mary Allen College Hospital. I kept my job after school began, working part time. This older nurse I mentioned earlier encouraged me to let Jimmie know I was pregnant. I told her that he said he loved me and wanted to marry me. I finally did as she asked and wrote him to let him know I was pregnant. He did not hesitate to contact me and before too long, came to Crockett to pick me up and bring me to Dallas. So I left school without telling my father where I was going. I kept imagining he would find me and kill me.

Chapter IV

Faithful is HE

This is the hard part for me to write. We were not married right away, because Jay was not divorced from his first wife. This I found out later. So we lived together until his divorce was final and we could get married. That was several years after he picked me up in Crockett. All our children were born before we were legally married. This has been a source of real shame for me down through the years. The only happy things are we have our five lovely children, and they all have the same father. This was very important to me all of my life, as I stated earlier. I appreciate Dr. and Mrs. Ruben Conner, who really stuck by me back then. Dr. Conner stayed on my husband until he got the divorce and his blood test. Then he married us in our own living room at 907 Grant Street in Dallas, with only Geneva Conner as a witness. There! I've said it. I was ashamed of the fact that I had "shacked" for so long, but it was beyond my control. I know one thing, I had no peace until this thing was completed. God has forgiven me for it, and I hope others will, also.

My life after our marriage was up and down. I was devoted to the Lord, my husband, family and Community Bible Church. We were a young church founded by Dr. Ruben Conner. (He was not a doctor then). Apart from my family, my church was the most important thing in my life. I really learned a lot about being a Christian and living a Godly life from Bro. Reuben, and all the teachers he exposed us to in our early years. I lived my life with an alcoholic husband for many years. We are the parents of seven living children. We lost two little girls very early and ended up with five children; three girls and two boys. My husband really loved me. He showed it in many ways. He taught me a lot of things about life. The first time I went shopping, I had all the wrong things in my basket like candy, cookies and sodas. He gently took everything out of the basket and told me, "Honey, we need to buy things like flour, meal, sugar, meat and potatoes." He also helped me to learn about city life and how to deal with people. When Jay and I first met, I had no idea he had a drinking problem, because he never let me see him in that state. He was very successful in keeping this important fact hidden from me. As our relationship progressed, I found out he had a very bad problem with alcohol.

We had a rocky life filled with ups and downs. My husband was a hard worker, but he was also a hard drinker. When I went into labor with our first child, he was drunk and our landlords (husband and wife) had to take me to the hospital. When they were finally able to sober him up, he came running. His love for me was real, it was just the addiction of alcohol was so strong, it superseded everything else. Our whole family was so hurt by his drinking. Our two sons had to carry him out of his car many a day because he was so drunk he could not get any further than the driveway. And sometimes one or the other of them had to do it alone. Sometimes he had to sleep on the floor, because he would fall down as soon as he came into the house. He was too heavy to lift onto the couch. I feel that the whole alcoholism bit caused me and our children to have some really bad personality problems. Thank God, since they have become adults, many of the problems seem to have evened out. At least we are all dealing with them.

Faithful is HE

My mother-in-law, Mama Vinie was so good to me. I remember when I was pregnant with Jackie, she sent LaRena Faye to stay with me. Rena would say, "Mama told me not to let you out of bed until the six weeks are up." Needless to say, I did as I was told because Rena had a heavy hand and didn't hesitate to use it. Mama Vinie was a good mother-in-law to me. She always took my side against Jay. We would have so much fun together. I was not a party person, because my father never let me go out when I was young. So when we would go to Greenville to visit her, I would mostly stay at home with her while Jay and his brothers went partying. We would cook, watch Charlie Chan movies and just talk. She would keep me laughing. She was naturally funny. I guess Jay took after his mother. Although, Jay, as he is sometimes called, was a hard drinker, he had many redeeming qualities. He was a hardworking man. He never missed work no matter how high he might have been the night before. If my husband stayed home from work, I knew he was really sick.

He brought his money home most of the time. Sometimes he didn't quite make it. In spite of the many times he "lost" his paycheck, God still saw to it that our children always had a roof over our-heads and food on the table. Thank you, Lord! Jay worked for the Lone Star Gas Company for 22 years and resigned. He worked with our friend, R. T. Johnson, for about 6 months after that. He then went to work for ITT Grinnell Company. He stayed there for about 21 years and retired. Grinnell gave him a steak dinner, the proverbial gold watch and a pension of $131. 00 per month. In our early years together, I worked in private homes, cleaning houses and taking care of children. After about two years, I, then, began to work for Golden Acres, a home for Jewish Aged. That was my first regular, company job. I worked there until I had our 4th child, Kimberly. I became pregnant with our last child, Tracy, right away, so I was unable to get another permanent job at that time.

My husband loved to be in the company of his friends. He loved to flash money and set his friends up with drinks. I think Jay was happiest when he had all his drinking buddies around him with plenty beer and Crown Royal whiskey. He would get high and start to tell jokes and stories. These parties most of the time lasted all night long. He thought nothing of staying out half the night many times corning home just in time to go to work the next morning. He was always so funny and could keep a person laughing with his jokes. There were times I wanted to be angry with him, but he would tell me a funny joke and I would start laughing, then the "mad" was over. He always had an audience. People would gather around him and listen to his many tall tales about his experiences in the marines and just about life. Many people said he reminded them of George Jefferson. My husband had a tender, loving side. At times, he was very gentle with our children. If they needed a splinter removed or a boil squeezed, they asked their dad. He could do it without causing them pain. I never saw anyone who could remove a splinter without the person experiencing the least bit of discomfort like my husband. I, in turn, could be so rough in handling it, the kids would say, "No, Mama, let daddy do it."

Faithful is HE

We had a great sex life. You can tell by all the children we had. Jay was very sweet to me. He knew how to make me feel like I was special. That is why I hated his drinking so much. I often told him, he had the potential to be such a great man, if he could only give up alcohol. He was smart, witty, congenial and made friends easily. All those good qualities were negated by his alcohol use. I remember one time when I went to Greenville, Texas to spend some time with Jay's mother, Mama Vinnie, a near tragedy occurred. It was right after we lost our third child, Tonia Yvette. (You will read more about her later in the book). I was gone several days to try to heal from Tonia's death. It seems that Jay went to bed drunk, got up, lit a cigarette and set the bed on fire. Our next-door neighbors, the Whitman's, heard his screams of terror. Mr. Whitman went over and was able to help him put out the fire. They told me that the mattress was burned all Around where Jay was sleeping. It was a miracle he wasn't burned to death or the house was not burned down. It seemed like a warning to Jay, but he paid no attention to the event. He was shook up for a while, but it didn't take long for him to go back to his old ways. In spite of his drinking, we did have our family times. Jay would take me and our children out to eat on some Friday nights. We would go to different kinds of restaurants such as Japanese, Chinese, etc. Whatever the kids ordered to eat, they had to finish it.

Jay would say, "Don't order anything unless you know what it is. If you order it, you eat it." So all our experiences were not bad ones. In our early years of marriage, my good friend, Geneva Conner, who I mentioned earlier, taught me and several other young women how to sew. She would have us to bring our portable sewing machines to her house on Berwick Avenue in Dallas. She had a kind of school going on. She showed us how to cut out garments together. There was Betty Price, Gloria Roberts and Zetha Phillips. Gen, as she is lovingly called, is a soft spoken, gentle woman. But she was not so gentle when she would tear our crooked seams apart and make us sew them straight. Boy, would we get mad when she did that. I know it was for our good. She was determined to teach me to sew, and it seemed I was just as determined to show her I could not learn. But I did learn. I learned so well I began making clothes for all my family. I am ever so grateful to Geneva for teaching me how to sew. I was able to save money by making school clothes instead of buying readymade fashions.

My husband also enjoyed my new-found skill of seamstress. I would make Jay jumpsuits out of loud-colored polyester fabric, then design headbands to match. He would change headbands when he changed jumpsuits. He thought he was the bomb. Everybody complemented him on his clothing. I also sewed for Jimmy Ray, our oldest son. He came up during the "Superfly" era. All the young, Black men wanted to dress like him even though he was not a good character. They wore topcoats past their knees, large brimmed hats, and shoes with high heels. I would pray over the pattern, then cut it out and put it together. Every suit came out perfect. God answered my prayer because I asked in faith, believing He would give me the "know how" to sew the garments. He would walk around proudly and say, "My Mama made my suit." I sincerely enjoyed sewing for my family, and because of the Lord and Geneva Conner, I did a pretty good job.

Jackie had me sewing special things for her. Now you know girls are so much harder to please than boys. So, when I made something for her and she liked it, I knew it was on. Once she wanted me to make a lined garment. I had never put a lining in anything. But when you have kids and they need something, most mothers will go out of their way to please them. So, I set out with much prayer over the pattern and went to work. It took me all night to finish it but finish it I did. It turned out great. When Jackie married at 18, I made her wedding dress. Nobody was more surprised than I was. Never in a million years would I have foreseen being able to sew just about anything I set my mind to. There was a time when I questioned my husband about God and life after death. I was so afraid of dying without knowing what it meant to be a true Christian. Jay could not give me any answers and would not try to find out, so he could help me. I remember feeling a hopelessness, wishing I knew more about Jesus and what He should mean to me. The traditional Baptist churches did not focus on Salvation by grace, so even though I attended church a lot, I still didn't learn about true salvation and what God should mean to me as a person, until I went to Community Bible Church.

I first went to Community Bible Church at 1227 Hendricks Avenue in October, 1963 during Halloween season. My kids and I went trick or treating down on Morrell Avenue. We stopped by Conner's Barber Shop for candy. We got the candy and an invitation to come to the formal opening of the new Community Bible Church building. We accepted the invitation and the rest is history. I soon became a member and raised my children at Community Bible Church under Dr. Ruben Conner, Pastor. I was 30 years old when I joined Community Bible Church in 1963. I had a bad smoking problem. By this time I had graduated from Winston's and Viceroys to the very strong Chesterfields and Raleigh's. I developed a persistent cough. The doctor told me that I had a spot on my lungs and needed to stop smoking. The first time I tried to stop, I quit for about four months. I began smoking again, and the coughing soon recurred. I was at my wits end and could not stop. I was up to two packs a day and opening another. It's hard to believe I ever smoked that many cigarettes in a week, let alone a day. Anyway, I spoke to Pastor Conner about my habit and he informed me that God could help me stop. At this point in my life, I had had no real experience with God and didn't know how God could help me stop smoking. All I ever heard in church was about Daniel in the lion's den, or Jonah in the whale, and David killing Goliath. I didn't have any idea what all that had to do with me.

Bro. Conner encouraged me to pray for deliverance, and to read a booklet he had about our bodies being God's temple and we should not defile them. I read the Scriptures and brochure and prayed. I did not believe in miracles. I just knew people who claimed miracles had happened to them were not begin truthful. Anyway, I began to pray sincerely for deliverance and began to believe God was concerned about my problem. One morning I had smoked about three cigarettes, but I was still praying. I cried out to my God with all my heart and He gave me a miracle. I would get on the piano and sing sometimes. That morning I couldn't stop singing "His Grace is Sufficient." Then like a lightning bolt from the sky, I felt the taste for cigarettes being taken from my body by the mighty hand of God in an instant. It was a miracle!! The miracle I needed to believe that God really loves me and was concerned about my problem. God removed the desire to smoke from my being once and for all. I was delivered from smoking in a moment. This was about 1964. I have not smoked since that day. When God does something, He does it well. He knew I needed a miracle and He gave me one. I'm still praising God for not smoking anymore!!!

My husband was really surprised. We always shared cigarettes, but now when he wanted me to smoke with him, I no longer had the desire. When I told him God delivered me from smoking, he didn't quite know what to say. I was smoking before he left that morning and had stopped by the time he came home. One thing I know, my husband loved me. He would not let anyone speak ill of me. I was His "Birdie," and you better not mess with me!. You better ax somebody!! Even through our trials and problems, I always knew he loved me and our children. The alcohol had the upper hand, and Jay was never able to give up and get help. When I was 39 years old, I began to think about my life's vocation. Time seemed to just fly by. One day all my five children were hovering around my feet. Before I knew it, they were growing up and in junior high and high school. We needed more money, so I applied for a grant to go to secretarial school. I felt that if I could learn a trade, I could get a better job and earn more money to help our family. I was approved for a grant to go to Rutherford's College of Business here in Dallas. It was about 1971. I chose a one-year course for becoming a professional secretary. As I stated earlier, I was 39 years old. It seemed to me I had to hurry and do something before I was 40.

The class I was in consisted of young people just out of high school. I was right in the middle of a bunch of kids. I was so sure I would not be able to keep up with them. I had been out of college over 25 years. But, guess what? I did better than they did, because I meant business and studied hard. Many days they would have to throw me out, so they could close the school. I would be practicing my typing or listening to tapes and taking short hand. Our classes were over at 1:00 p.m. and they closed the school about 3:00 p.m., so I used that time in between to practice. We started out with a class of about 20 students. After our year's training, we ended up with five students. But that was all right. We could all type our required 65 words per minute and take shorthand at 120 w.p.m. When I started out, I did not believe I would ever type or take shorthand that fast. That just shows if we trust God, strive and work hard, we can reach any goal.

My first job after graduating was with a local Black newspaper called the Dallas Express. I was so happy to be able to type, file and take care of their business. I only worked there for about 1 year. Then I started to work for Bro. Ruben Conner, my pastor at the time. It was only part-time. I worked for him about three or four years. The time came when we really needed more money for our kids. I applied to the Dallas Independent School District for a Secretarial position at a senior high school. Since I was able to meet the qualifications, I got the job. I had to leave Bro. Conner for the public schools. My first school was Lincoln High School. I began work there in 1974 under Dr. Frederick D. Todd. Dr. Todd was the only principal I worked for that knew how to do payroll and every other secretarial duty. He taught me how to be a secretary. I really appreciate him for that. He also gave me a good evaluation when he left at the end of 74. That way I could continue working without having to worry about my status with the District.

We would all get a big kick out of Dr. Todd walking around singing old songs we knew way back when I was a child, like " Gimmie back that wig I bought you and let your head go bald," and "There ain't nobody here but us chickens, by Louis Jordan. Dr. Todd left Lincoln after my first year, and Dr. Harold Lang came in 1975. Everybody told me that he was going to be really hard to work for. I found him to be just the opposite. He was great to work for. He was the kind of administrator that knew what he wanted to say and said he. He wrote out all his letters fully. All I had to do was type them up. He also worked a lot on the plans for the new Lincoln High School. Dr. Lang was principal from 1975 till 1980. He was a very learned man. I believe he told me he was among the first Blacks to get-a doctorate from North Texas State University. People came from all over the District to ask his advice about different things. He got sick in February with some type of heart condition and died on February 14, 1980. It was a real shock for all of us. He had called me about three days before to say he would be in to work on Monday.

I really missed Dr. Lang. He had so much to offer the city and the world. He had started to write a book about Jesse Jackson, whom he admired with a passion. I was helping him by typing up his script after school as he wrote. I really hate I did not keep a copy of his writings. I believe they would be valuable today. One month after Dr. Lang's death the District hired Dr. Napoleon Lewis to be the principal of Lincoln High School. We had a good relationship to begin with, but after a while things changed. I worked with Dr. Lewis for 5 years. Then at some point, he asked me to find me another position. I was really hurt because I loved Lincoln High School. It was my first school, and all the people who worked there seemed like my extended family. While I was still at Lincoln in April of 1980, tragedy struck our family. My daughter Kim had married a young man named Phillip Michael Payne. He was a good boy, just misled. She was very young, 17 or 18 years old. They had a little boy named Phillip, Jr. Their relationship was rocky at best. Phillip drank and was violent toward her at times, but we loved him and tried to help them with their marriage.

Faithful is HE

One-night Kim and Phillip went to a party and Phillip got drunk or high on drugs or something. Anyway, he came to our house late to get Kim and Little Phillip and he was stoned. Kim had come to our house after the party, even though they had their own apartment. I think Kim was a little afraid of Phillip when he was drinking. Anyway, one thing led to another and Phillip attacked Jay. I asked Tracy, our baby daughter, to call the police. Before the police could get to the house Phillip had attacked Jay again and Jay had shot him. I think the bullet went right through his heart. I saw blood coming out of his mouth and pouring out of his shirt near his heart. Somehow, I knew that Phillip was dead even before the ambulance came. The picture is still in my mind even after all these years. That event will go with me to my grave. The intensity of it stayed with me for many years.

Jay and I loved Phillip and he loved us. The drugs he ingested changed his personality completely. Earlier that day, Jay and Phillip had been riding around together enjoying each other. Something made Phillip change and become totally different. I sincerely regret Jay felt he had to shoot Phillip. Jay said later he was afraid in Phillip's state of mind, he might take the gun and shoot us all. The paramedics came and took him to Parkland Hospital, he died several hours later. Now our daughter, Kim, had to raise their son without his father. All of us who were present when Phillip was shot were questioned by the police. Since we all told the same story, the truth, Jay never had to serve any time for the shooting. It was ruled as self-defense. But the emptiness in our lives remained and still does with the loss of our dear son-in-law. God rest his soul. That night twenty years ago will remain in my memory forever.

In 1984, Dr. Lewis told me to find another school to work at. In other words, leave Lincoln. I couldn't believe it. I had worked so hard for him and received excellent ratings, so I did not know what to do. I frantically called my friend, Myrtle Salone, who had retired as registrar of Lincoln. We were close. We had experienced some bad times with Dr. Lewis. It drew us closer together. His wife, Mrs. Nell Lewis was very sympathetic with me. She was so kind to me when I had a bad day with Dr. Lewis. Myrt, as we called her, helped me through that hurting period. The time soon came when I did find another position at Health Special High School. The Lincoln staff bought me a cake, made a little punch and said "Goodbye, Birdie, it's been nice knowing you," just like all my hard work meant nothing. I felt like a castaway. I had done much of the hard work of moving us from the old building to the new building and setting everything up to begin school in the new Lincoln High School building located right next to the old building. That was a good lesson for me and everyone who reads this, we can all be replaced, not matter how good we think we are.

I guess I thought Lincoln could not run without me. I did make some lasting friends at Lincoln. Ms. Wilma Bennett was in the office with me. She had been at Lincoln several years before I was hired. We formed a great friendship. Our first and second grand children were born the same year. We are also close to the same age. We had a lot in common. We kept in touch even after I left Lincoln, and still do.

There was Hassell Tanksley, who was an assistant principal. He was my good friend and advisor. Hassell passed away about 5 years ago. I really appreciated him and all he meant to the school. It's so sad that many times great men or women are never given a thank-you for all their good deeds. I don't want to leave out Henry Roddy. He was the Dean of Instruction at one time. We have kept in touch. He and his wife, Camille, moved to Little Rock, Arkansas. Once they sent for me to come there to render music at a special meeting. It was extremely enjoyable, and Little Rock is a beautiful city. Camille is one of the best cooks I ever met. She would make biscuits from scratch that made you want to slap your preacher, and she loves cooking like Henry loves eating. I also fell in love with their little daughter, Millett. I claimed her for one of my little grandchildren. We still keep in touch.

I spent the next 11 years at Health Special High School, a school for pregnant teens. Mrs. Pearlie Wallace was my principal. We took a liking to each other right away. I was a lot older than Mrs. Wallace, so some the faculty said I acted like her mother. We were like a family at Health Special in those early years. That is when I truly realized no matter what color we are, we are all basically the same. We cry when we hurt, our men whether Black or White, mess up and cheat on us. We get angry and over react at times, and so on. We developed a kinship between Black, White, Hispanic, and Asian, that still exists. I had to adjust to seeing only pregnant girls. Up to that point, I had spent 10 years Around "good students," many of whom wanted to excel, having programs about excellence, etc. Now, here I was dealing with young women who were at their worst. There were girls as young as 12 and 13 years old, pregnant. It made me depressed for a while. I soon got used to it and did my best to encourage them to go ahead in spite of their circumstances.

As it is with all jobs, we had our ups and downs, but I can say, on a whole, it was a good time in my life. I came in contact with wonderful staff members like: Staphalene Hunter, Brenda Evans, Hazel Jackson, Jane Passmore, Darlene Fincannon, Billie Betts, Nita Moorehead, Claudia Swain, Shirley Ware, David Drysdale, Judy Bryant, Portia Tucker, Richard Campbell, Edna Sue Ferguson, Brenda Baxter, Robert Searight, and so many others. If I missed a friend's name from Health Special, please forgive me. One event in my life I will remember forever. Is the day I lost my mother, March 7, 1992. My sisters and I put mom in the South Dallas Nursing Home about 2 years earlier. She was fine for about 2 1/2 years.

Then she got very sick with congestive heart failure. We were told she did not have long to live. So, we engaged hospice services for her. On the day of her death (March 9, 1992), I had been to the nursing home and gone back to work. I had only been back to work a short while when I got a call that mother was dying. I was so shook up I could not drive, so our reading teacher, Dr. Claudia Swain, volunteered to drive me. She stayed with me until my mom passed away. She didn't say anything at all, but she was there. That meant so much to me for her to stay with me all that time. I will always be grateful to Dr. Swain for being there for me in such an intense time of need.

Chapter V

Faithful is HE

In 1995, I began to get tired of the work I was doing. The bureaucracy and politics of the District began to get to me. I prayed to God for an answer as to whether I should retire or not. I had done my research and was able to take full retirement at age 62 after 21 years of service to the Dallas Independent School District. The Lord did answer yes, it was indeed time. I gave my proper notices on time. Mrs. Wallace and the Health Special staff gave me a big retirement party. I will always be grateful for the elaborate send-off, and all of the nice gifts I received. I still have some of the memorabilia given to me at that time.

Speaking of elaborate parties, my kids gave me a wonderful 62nd birthday party. On August 1, 1995, they gave me my first surprise birthday party. It was a grand affair and I have never been more surprised about anything. They had the party at the De Soto, Texas Civic Center. They invited my friends from work, Community Bible Church and my new church home, These Are They Community Church. At that party, I met my new daughter-in-law to be, Stephanie Taylor. Would you believe we were wearing the same dress, even though mine was a 24 and hers was probably a 7 or 8. I thank God for that special day my children planned for me.

Before I tell you about my husband's stroke, I would like to write a little bit about our children and some of the things they went through. I feel it is significant to my total project. Our oldest son, Jimmy Ray (named for his dad and uncle) had a very hard life. He became rebellious right after junior high school. He developed a drinking problem early in life. I remember when he was about 3 years old, Jay would sit at the table with a beer in front of him and one in front of Ray. I did not want Jay to give Ray beer, but he insisted on doing so. He thought it was funny. I didn't know what to do. I just knew it wasn't right. All through Ray's young life, Jay gave him beer. Later in life, Jay refused to take any responsibility for Ray's alcoholism. In his teen years, Ray became an alcoholic, and subsequently, an addict. There was a time when I did not want to see my son coming. He acted so strangely when he was "under the influence." But, no matter how high he became, he always respected me as his mother. I remember one time he came to the house high on drugs, and I got so mad I grabbed a big stick to hit him. He said, "Go ahead and hit me, mama, I deserve it." I didn't hit him. It hurt me so badly to see my oldest son following in his father's footsteps.

Needless to say, I was very happy when my son came to me and told me he had had a spiritual experience, and he no longer desired to drink or do drugs. I held my breath for a while because I didn't know if it was real or not. It did turn out to be real. He became so committed, he stopped smoking and eating meat. He is now a vegetarian and a licensed fitness trainer. Look at the work of our Lord!! Ray was once married to Glenda Joyce Ross and they had one son, Steven. Steven has two children: Little Stevie and Zekia. Ray was also married to Janet Shaw for a time. They had no children together, but her two children B.J. and Tenet were dear to me. She is a sweet lady and a top-flight beautician. He was married to Juvanda and she had a son named Drayton. That marriage lasted about 3 months. I was very fond of Juvanda and Drayton. He has a daughter, Shenequa Burshea Washington, who we call Shea. Her mother is Arlesia Washington. We are all very proud of Shea who completed her college education at Texas A & M University last year. I know people have to take responsibility for their own actions, but, I sincerely believe Ray would have had a better child hood if Jay had been a different kind of father. As he often says, he had no positive male influence in his life as he grew up. This can have a damaging effect on anyone.

In a family as large as mine and Jay's there was not one man who ever opened a Bible and taught the children of the family. That is a very poor testimony for any family. However, Dr. Conner taught us how to teach the Bible to our children. I had to be the Spiritual leader in our family. We had regular devotions in our home, also we invited the neighborhood children to be in on them.

Jacquelyn, our second child and first daughter, was a joy from birth. She always loved her mommy and would cry when I left her with a sitter. I kidded her later in life by telling her, "You used to love me a lot and cry for me." She would say, "I still love you, mama." This girl had and still has a mind of her own. She has the tenacity of a bull dog. Once she makes up her mind about something, it takes almost an act of congress to get her to change it. I remember when we moved from Oak Cliff to College Park (Out near Bishop College). I believe this was her first year in high school. She would have been going to Roosevelt High School. She had gone to Roger Q. Mills Elementary School, and Oliver Wendell Holmes Junior High School from the 1st grade to the 8th grade. All the friends she made during those years would be going to Roosevelt, and of course, she wanted to be with them. This was a crushing blow to have to change schools, and make new friends, and all that goes with moving.

Jacquelyn became so ill, I was frightened for her. I did not realize until then how young people's issues that seem so trivial to adults, are so very important to them. This is the truth. Jacquelyn would not eat, she lost weight, (she was already really tiny) and just lay in bed and stared at the ceiling. I didn't know what to do. I even went to some important officials to try to get her in Roosevelt, but to no avail. The only way I could get her in Roosevelt was to pay tuition. With a family of seven, and limited funds, that was not possible. As a Christian, I was praying all along the Lord would give me wisdom in dealing with this issue. I hope my memories of this incident are correct. After trying everything I knew to do, I gave lip and told her she would have to go to Wilmer Hutchins High School. Jacquelyn didn't really want to go to another high school, but she went on since it was the only thing to do. As time went on, she made friends and began to feel better about going. God is so faithful! That Is why I wanted to write this book to emphasize how God intervenes when things are bad and makes good out of them.

Back to Jacquelyn. When she was a junior in high school, she ran for Miss Wilmer Hutchins High School. During the contest, she sang a medley of Negro Spirituals consisting of: "Talk About A Child That Do Love Jesus, I Want Jesus To Walk With Me and Soona Will Be Done With The Trouble of the World." She won over girls who may have had better voices, but they sang secular songs. Jackie was so sincere as she sang, she had the students and teachers crying. I believe God allowed her to win to help her through the trauma of leaving her neighborhood school. He is so faithful, even in our so called "little things."

Jacquelyn married right out of high school to Jessie McClellan, and had our first grandchild, Carla Nikol, who was such a joy to Jay and me. In fact, Jay was so crazy about Carla he and Jackie were at odds constantly about her care and etc. He even tried to keep her with us when Jackie moved out to get her own apartment. I need to explain, Jackie's marriage to Jessie did not work out, so she moved back home until she was able to get her own apartment. During that time, Jay really got crazy about Carla. She was the best thing that had ever happened to us. Since this book is about my life, I won't write extensively about my children. I mainly wanted to show how God has worked in our lives down through the years. So, I'll just give you short glimpses of their lives.

When Carla was about 5 or 6 years old, Jackie met the man of her dreams and ours, too (Jay's and mine). He loved Jackie and Carla and us. He was kind to our daughter and a good provider. We didn't lose a daughter, we gained a son. He has been the same after all these years ... steady and dependable. Thank God for sending Robert Joe Lacy into our family. He has always felt like a true son. I can call on him whenever I need him, and he will do whatever I need done. They have since had a son, Jorell, who is the image of his dad and his paternal grandparents, Dale and Katy Lacy, and their other sons Bobby and Rickey. They are a happy, loving family, trusting the Lord daily. We are so proud of Carla. She got her bachelor's degree about two years ago, and her masters about a year and a half ago. She is the first one in our family to graduate from college. Jarrell finished high school this year and is going to college. Hallelujah! ! ! Jacque', as she now calls herself, is a good example for her daughter and other young ladies she is around. She loves the Lord and is active in His work through These Are They Community Church. She is truly a daughter to be proud of.

We had a little girl named Tonia Yvette before we had Jeff, she lived to be 17 months old. She died with what is called A-Plastic Anemia. She started out bleeding from her gums. By the time she died, she was bleeding from her ears, rectum and vagina. It seems the condition results from a malformation of the blood corpuses. The blood then is unable to coagulate, thus causing profuse bleeding. They did not have a cure then. They just kind of experimented on different drugs to give her relief. I have since learned they now give bone marrow transplants to A-Plastic Anemia patients. That was the first time either Jay or I had experienced a death so close in our family. It was a very hurting time in our lives. My sister, Erma Jean was living with us at the time. She loved Tonia like her own. We were all devastated by Tonia's death, but I believe my sister Erma Jean was more torn up than anyone.

Erma came to live with us when she was 16 years old and pregnant. I was 25 years old and had no idea what to do with a 16-year-old person. Our mother could not seem to deal with my sister, even though she (mother) was very promiscuous when she was young. I found that very strange. So, I did not try to stop Erma from making Tonia almost her whole life. It seemed I was glad she found joy in something, because she was a very sad and troubled girl at that time. Later in her life, Erma did get her life together. She lost the first child, but subsequently, had two other children, my niece, Marian and nephew, Antonio Claude. Jean married Raymond Hornbuckle and they have a son, Raymond, Jr. Jean also went to trade school and learned to be respiratory therapist. She now practices at several different hospitals. At the time of Tonia's death, I was pregnant with our fourth child. This child would have been born in April as our other three children had been. You see we had a pattern, Jay and me. He would have his vacation every July, and I had a baby every April for four consecutive years. I guess the strain of losing Tonia, caused my insides to rebel, and I had a miscarriage. It happened when I was in a phone booth calling a lady I was working for at the time. She was going to buy Tonia's burial clothing, and I was giving her funeral information on the telephone. All at once I felt something warm and wet flowing from me. I looked down and there in the phone booth, was a huge amount of blood, tissue and everything. Was I scared! I really hated to leave that mess there, but I was so weak from the loss of blood I had no choice but to leave and get home as fast as possible. I often wondered what happened when the next person came into that phone booth to use the phone!

Albert Jeffrey, our third, living child, is a very talented and bright young man, very computer literate. He has had the misfortune of being married several times. I won't go into the marriages. I just know I tried to raise my children by God's standards. How they turned out is up to the Lord and them. He is a kind; soft spoken man. Only the Lord knows why he had so much marital trouble. He now lives with me and is a great help to me, financially and mentally. He also has two young sons, Alex and J.J. II, along with his two older daughters Shantel and Shayla. The mother of the girls is his first wife, Valerie, and the mother of the boys is Felicia King, a very kind and gentle young lady. He was also married to Deborah Kimble and is now married to Stephanie Taylor. Both are very nice young ladies.

We had another little girl named Regina Kim. Regina was born before Kimberly. She only lived three months. My husband laid on her and smothered her. I was working at night then, and when I came home, I put her in the bed with us. I should have been more careful and placed her on the left side of me instead of in the middle of us. My husband inadvertently laid his shoulder over her face in his sleep.

When I awoke that morning, she was under his shoulder still and cold. Oh, so sickeningly still. I tried to revive her, but to no avail. I called the fire department, which was just down the block from us. They came quickly and tried to revive her, but it was too late. That was a very hurting time for our family. Regina was a beautiful child. When I brought her home after she was born, I would stare at her while she was asleep. I felt in my bones we would not have that baby long. Sometimes it seemed like I could see a light around her, like she was a little angel. We had no pictures made of her, but Jay and I both remember her as being a beautiful baby.

I never told Jay I found Regina under his shoulder, neither did I tell the firemen. I just told them when I woke up, I found her not breathing. She had a bad cold and was very congested, so the cause of her death was ruled as pneumonia. I did not feel Jay could have mentally handled such a load. Kimberly Michelle Houston-Payne-Dillard-Johnson is our 4th child. She was born on November 12, 1961 and was a somewhat troubled child growing up. It might have been because she was what is called a "knee baby." That is the baby next to the last child. She was unable to be the baby for long.

I had our last child, Tracy Laverne, when Kimberly was 10 months old. She had to make way for the last child. She was not walking when Tracy was born. But she started soon afterward. I won't go into the trials of our daughter's life. She has been in recovery for 9 years. Needless to say, we are thankful for that. She has two sons, Phillip and Deandre, and is holding her own. Phillip has a son, Little Phil, who is a year old. His mother is Kokila Eaton. Tracy Laverne is our last child. She was born in September 23, 1962. When I was pregnant with her, I was the meanest person even I ever knew, as I look back. I stayed at home all the time. Didn't go to church, drank beer and fought my husband. Up to this time, I was not a drinker. But, while pregnant with Tracy, I somehow acquired a taste for beer.

I have to give it to my husband. He was there for me at that time. I would just start fighting him for no reason. It seemed I hated him. I don't know what happened to me. I would throw things at him, curse him out for not bringing my quart of beer when he came home from work. I guess I was angry at him because I stayed pregnant all the time. I had gone to the doctor to get my tubes tied, but the doctor said, "Mrs. Houston, we can't tie your tubes, because you are already pregnant." I was so tired of having babies by this time. Talk about keeping me barefoot and pregnant! That seemed to be Jay's greatest goal in life. I stayed home, had babies, cooked and cleaned for him while he ran the streets with his friends. That was the story of our lives in those days. I don't want my baby, Tracy, to think we didn't want her. It's just that our timing was the worst in the world. Kim was only 10 months old, and the other kids were still babies and needing so much care.

Faithful is HE

I don't know if my behavior while pregnant with her, accounts for the moodiness of Tracy or not. But I did read somewhere, the demeanor you exhibit while carrying your child can sometimes be passed on to the child. Tracy has three children. She married Karl Wynne several years ago. They are separated at the present time. But I hope they will one day be reconciled. Her daughter, Nytosha gave birth to my first great grandchild, "Nyteara Kenyla." She now has a little boy named Derrick, II. Tracy's other children are Damonte' and Karl, Jr.

Chapter VI

Faithful is HE

In July 1995, my sweetheart, Jay had a stroke on his right side. He has been paralyzed ever since. I had just retired a month before he had his stroke. I had prayed and asked God if I should retire and His answer was yes. With good reason, too. I retired in June of 95, and Jay had a stroke in July of 95. Look at God's timing! If I had still been at work, I would have been unable to care for him as I should have. But the Lord led me to go ahead and retire. That tells us we should always consult the Lord about our life's decisions. Proverbs 3:5 - 6. "Trust in the Lord with all your heart and lean not to your own understanding. In all your ways acknowledge Him and He will direct your path.", are the verses that guide my life. The family went through a lot of trauma during Jay's illness. The Lord was taking us through things we had no idea how to handle. But He handled them for us. Jay was in the Veteran's Hospital for about 3 months. Then he was transferred to the TCU. That is the Transitional Care Unit at the Veterans Hospital. He was there for one year. They taught him how to handle himself in a wheel chair, how to transfer from chair to car, chair to bed, chair to toilet. It is really amazing how much they helped him.

All this was so new to me and the children. Here was my husband, a tough, old marine, always his own man, doing for himself and us, now unable to speak or to really help himself very much. It was truly an adjustment for us all. I kept Jay at home for a year. During that time, I had help from Home Health Care Aides. After the year was up, new laws were put on the books that limited home health care to certain persons. We lost our home health care. I took care of my husband for 6 months without help. After 6 months, I began to feel the strain of the 24-7 care of a disabled adult. I'm almost four years younger than my husband, but, nevertheless, still growing old, and unable to stand the strain of caring for him. I began to cry a lot and become depressed. My husband became more belligerent. He resented my going out, but would not go out with me, even when I begged him to. He did not try to help himself, so he could still enjoy life. I wanted him to go riding with me in the car. He refused to leave the house unless I told him he had a doctor's appointment. He even fought me at times, which was really out of character for him. Before his stroke, he would never hit me and was mad at any man who hit a woman, if he knew about it.

He would hide his social security checks, if they came when I was out. I would ask "Honey, did your social security check come?" With a straight face he would shake his head "no." I knew He was lying because there's one thing you can say about the government, Those S.S. checks come right on time and sometimes before the 3rd. I would tell Jay "I'm going to call Ray to come over, if you don't show me where the check is." It was funny. He would mouth obscenities to me like "f-you." But after a few minutes he would go to where he had hidden his check and give it to me. Ray and I often laughed about this. The roles were reversed. Now he feared Ray. In the early years, it was the other way around. The decision to place my husband in a nursing home was the hardest one I've ever had to face. I began to think about it after 6 months of caring for him alone. I went round and round in my mind about it. You know what a stigma Black folks put on nursing homes. So here I was trying to come to grips with placing Jay. I truly love my husband and it was an agonizing time for me. My kids were all supportive, but they had their own families, jobs and lives. I felt like a traitor. Here is the man I've pledged to love, honor, and obey, to be with him in sickness and health, for richer or for poorer, for better or for worse, till death do us part. And I'm thinking of putting him in a nursing home.

I mulled over this situation for many a day. There was a time when I enrolled Jay in an adult day care center. He went for a while, but then he got where he just would not leave the house. He would hold on to furniture to keep me from wheeling him out of the house. I was working part time as a substitute in the Dallas Public Schools. I could not leave him home alone for very long. Once while he was doing well getting his food from the ice box. I would fix him a cold lunch, show him what is was and where I was placing it in the ice box. When I came home, I found he was getting it and eating. But after a while, he stopped doing it. He would wait until I came home to eat. Sometimes he would open the door and call the kids in the neighborhood to come help him. That wasn't so bad. But when he started calling strangers in to help him, I got really concerned.

One day he called two strange men into the house. It just so happened that Kokila, a young lady that was courting my grandson, Phillip, was walking down the street and saw a dog on my porch. Since I don't have a dog, she went in and investigated. Kokila found one man in our bedroom looking at our belongings like he was going to help himself the other man was in kitchen helping Jay. Kokila said she told them to get out of Nanny's house. One man said "Who is Nanny.? She knew then they were strangers because everybody in the neighborhood calls me Nanny. They got it from my grandchildren who started calling me Nanny when they were very young. That was the last straw. He let strangers in the house, he refused to leave the house, would not go to the day care center. He sometimes had moods that made him want to fight me, his wife, who loved him and was his caregiver. All these factors put together convinced me it was time for a drastic change.

I have cried a many night missing my husband and being sorry that I had to place him in a home. Only God has given me consolation about it. I realize I cannot take care of him alone. So, I try to take as good care of his needs as possible in the facility. I want to give special thanks to my brother-in-law, Robert T. Mosley and his wife Edith. Edith is the youngest sister to Jay. Robert and Jay have a special bond. It was formed before Jay got sick. Since Jay had his stroke, Robert T. has been right there to help. He gives Jay his haircuts and brings him a pound of Bar B Que ribs periodically (as if my little fat husband needs ribs), cases of his favorite sodas, and boxes of cookies and cakes. He is there to help us any way he can, and I appreciate Edith also for being there for us. For a while, Jay was very angry with me for placing him there. When I would go to visit him, he would turn his face in anger from me. His eyes looked at me accusingly. It was hard to face him. He has gotten better. He will sometimes smile and hold my hand. I sincerely hope that in his heart, with what reasoning is left after the stroke, he knows how much it hurt me to have to let him go to the home.

As I wrote at the beginning of my story, I was a member of Community Bible Church for almost 30 years. We had two bad splits. I finally left with the second split. I won't go into details, but I sincerely felt the Lord leading me the way I went. I left with the second pastor after Dr. Conner retired. His name is Rev. Willie J. Bolden. It was very hard to leave my church. I had spent most of my young years there. Dr. Conner had been my spiritual mentor. We learned basic and advanced Scriptural principles under his teachings. We memorized so many verses, most of the verses I still remember. There were so many of my good friends I hated to leave. I cried many nights about leaving. I had so many good friends like Oretha Johnson, and her daughter Beverly Smith, who is like our oldest daughter. Beverly's two children are Jay's and My god children. They are Regina and Wade Wende' Smith. Her husband, Big Wade, one of Jay's good friends. Regina now has two girls named Charlene and Evelyn. Wende' daughter's name is Stacia. Wende' is now married to a young lady named Kim.

Beverly and I have been friends and running buddies for many years. When Regina and Wende' were little children 4 and 5 years old, we used to go shopping for them and us. Beverly is kind of bossy. We all kid her about making us do what she wants us to do. She would insist that I put clothes in the lay-away to wear to work. It was a good idea, so I did it. The kids would pick out their own clothes at that young age, and were very particular about what they ate. It was the first time I saw little children so opinionated. We remain friends until this day, and always find time to go shopping or out to eat when she has vacation from her job at the Dallas Public Schools. We keep in touch and call each other when we need special prayer about things going on in our lives. Needless to say, I was sorry to leave Oretha, Beverly, Timothy and Felicia (Oretha's other children). I met Oretha when Beverly was about 18 years old. So, we've been friends for a very long time.

Some of my other friends at Community Bible Church are: Booker and Shirley Green, Myrtle Warner, Louis and Carolyn Peterson, Christina; Walter and Liz Drake. I played for both the Drake's and the Peterson's weddings. I appreciate Irene Ridge, John and Brenda Dodd, Louis and Minnie Franklin, Sister Celestine Fuller, all the Conner children, John and Sharon Avery, and of course Doc and Geneva Conner. I remember when Leon Moore proposed to Joyce, and I played for their wedding; the William Askew's, the Boles, Gail Johnson, the Else family, Caroline and her children. Ola Redmond and Margarette Galloway. Ray and Betty Price and their children, and Katrel and Gloria Roberts (before they left Community). My, we went through so many rough and good times together. I can't call everybody's name, but I love all my friends at Community Bible Church. Many of the young people who are grownups now were in my kindergarten class when C.B.C. was located on Hendricks Avenue. Some of whom are: All the Conner children, the Willis children Carlton, Bambi and Stacy Smith, Elvira Green, Yolanda, Andre And Monique Ridge, Rodney Ridge, Marietha Sands, Tim Johnson and many more. I loved those children, and we had great times together. God was truly with us as we taught His Word to the children. The Welfare Department was against us teaching the children to memorize Scripture, but God prevailed and we kept on teaching His Word, and encouraging the children to memorize scripture verses. We all went through some trying times at Community Bible Church. But thank God we have come through. The Lord has blessed Community and our church which is called "These Are They Community Church.

At this point I want to mention my relationship with the second pastor of Community Bible Church, Rev. Ralph V. Clark. He, Karen and their children came after Dr. Conner retired. I really appreciate Pastor Clark. He left Community after about 5 years, but not on real good terms. I did him a great injustice by signing a petition against him, even though I did not pray about it. After everything was over, I asked him for forgiveness and he forgave me without any hesitation. I love and respect several members who left with him and who are still good friends: Mother Edna Kelley (great, great grandmother of Nyteara), Elmer and Sandra Taylor, The Smiths, Austin and Caroline Kelley (grandparents of my great granddaughter, Nyteara), and many others. Many thanks to the Clarks for being so understanding towards me. They really exhibited the love of God by forgiving me so completely. May God continuously bless them and their church Agape Bible Church. I want to also mention Steve and Shirley Jones, who left Community with T.A.T. They were good friends of Jay's and mine. Steve is a good Bible teacher and Shirley is still a good friend.

When Pastor Bolden became pastor of Community Bible Church, I had already retired as musician after 30 years of service. A young lady, named Jeanie Johnson became our new musician. I met Jeanie at a Women's retreat in Conroe, Texas. I remember when I first saw her and her sister, Joan Sutton, singing together. I had never heard of either of them. They sang so beautifully together. I don't recall if we even talked at the retreat. I do know that somehow, we met, talked and clicked. Later on, I found out we were born on the same month and day, August 1. We had so much in common, the most important thing was our mutual love for the Lord and respect for each other. We are both church musicians. Jeanie is a super musician and anointed of God in her playing, singing and Bible teaching. We became friends and talked together about our families. She began playing for C.B.C. right after Bro. Bolden became pastor. We began to share our innermost thoughts and dreams for our children. Not much later, we became real friends.

We really tried to fix some of the things that were wrong at Community while Pastor Bolden was there. But evidently, it was not for us to remain. So as a result, several of us left with Pastor Bolden in October 1993. They were: Loretta Bolden and her two children, Faye Nobles, Mary Jackson and daughter, Joe and Jackie Lacy and their two children, Jimmie Jay, Jimmy Ray, Kimberly Payne, Karl and Tracy Wynne, Victor Jackson, Steve and Shirley Jones, Alfred and Jeanie Johnson, their children, Toni and Greg Johnson, Joe and Desiree Terry and their three children, Calvin and Gail Hall and their three children, Joyce Earl (a very dear and sweet young lady), Helen Allen, Sharon Edwards with Mother Marvella, Marna Helen, Michael and Donna Lee, Oscar and Michelle Taylor, Reginald Carter, and April Tisdale. Some others who left with us are: Loretta Holman and Jason, Rose Davis, Eva Harrison, Benny and Nancy Williams, Shonda Aime, Levi Ferris, Karen White, O.T. Williams, Dorcas and John House, Levi Ferris, and Michael and Denice Randell. I may have left out some names, but these are the majority of the ones who left Community Bible Church in 1993.

Jeanie and I are still close friends and prayer partners. We have been praying on Sunday nights for the past four years. In those four years I don't think we have missed more than three times praying. For about two of those years, Shirley Jones was a third in the prayer circle, but about two years ago, she and her husband, Steve, left our congregation. And later, several other people left us, but God has prevailed, and we are still going full force, and just about to build.

Chapter VII

Faithful is HE

Not long after that, Shirley became unable to pray with us anymore, but she has remained a good friend and we talk occasionally and keep in touch. Nevertheless, God has done some mighty works through Jeanie's and my prayers. We can talk to each other about anything. You don't get too many of those kinds of friends in a lifetime. Jeanie's husband, Alfred, was so kind to keep my little "Ms. Priss," my 1991 Prism, running like a top. I really appreciate how he helped me by just charging me for the parts. Ms. Priss was always running. I love her children Toni and Greg. They are great kids and always treat me with the utmost respect and care. I was blessed with a newer car, a 1997 Oldsmobile, a few months ago. Alfred told me not get a car unless it was a General Motors car, since he does not work on foreign models. Needless to say, I purchased another G.M. car.

At the present moment, our church worships at Southwest Baptist Church on Beltline Road. We have had our ups and downs as most churches do. But the Lord has kept a remnant together. We have begun to build on our land on Polk and Beltline. I love my pastor, Bro. Bolden and his lovely wife, Loretta. We have become very close these last four years. They have sweet children Cymone and Courtney. His older children by his deceased wife, Sondra, are good kids: Marcus, Talitha and Joseph. I really think a lot of them all and miss them since they left Dallas. I also love and appreciate my deaconess sisters: Dianne Byrd, Donna Lee, Jacque Lacy (my daughter), Rose Davis, Michelle Taylor, Ramona Jackson, Jeanie Johnson, Mary Jackson, and Faye Nobles. Also, Uncle Pete, Ms Ollie Cooper, Cecil and Cora Ford,

Ouida Hale, Weta Sweat and her daughters, Barbara and Lisa, and many others. It's hard to name everybody. I don't want to leave out Victor Jackson and Michael Lee, Robert and Loretta Goodman, the two Hazels, Ms. Hazel Carter's new husband and Mrs. Hazel Fingers. I have really learned to love them all.

I wanted to write my story for my children, so they will know God has been very real in my life since I was very young. He bought me out of "a horrible pit, out of the miry clay, and set my feet upon a rock.". Psalms 40: verse 2. I want to give glory to God for my husband. I know he had his problems with alcohol and other things, but as I look back on our lives, I can say this: My husband always kept a roof over our heads, he went to work every day, if we had hungry days, I don't think I or my children can remember them, we had some good times as a family, going out to eat and fun at home. God gave me the grace to stay with my husband in spite of the hard times and I'm so glad I did.

I was his "Birdie" and he did his best to take care of me and his children. Because he worked hard and paid into Social Security for many years, I am able to pay bills and be self-sufficient. I thank God for Jimmie Jay Houston being my husband for 45 years. I'd like to give props to Pastor Ruben Conner. In our early years of marriage when the really hard times came, I wanted to leave my husband. I would call Bro. Conner for help. I wanted him to agree with me about leaving, but he would always tell me what the Word said. He would say, "Sister Houston, if you leave your husband, you will be out of the will of God. If he does not abuse you and if he provides for you, you must trust God to bring you through these difficult times." I most certainly did not want to be out of the will of God, so I stayed with my husband and God did work things out for us. Maybe not like I thought He should, but the way He had planned for me. That is why I can say to younger married couples that if you trust God with your marriage, He will be faithful and bring you out successfully. It's only when we try to fix things ourselves that we get into trouble.

I have a painful injection at this time. I had almost forgotten about the abuse I suffered at the hands of a woman who was a friend of my mother. I won't mention her name, but she was very ·cunning person. She pretended to be my mother's friend, but I recall times when she would take me into a room, lock the room and make me put my mouth on her vagina. I remember her placing a towel near her, so I could spit. I did not know what to do about this. There was no one to talk to. I was about 11 or 12 years old. I don't believe people even had any inkling these things were going on. Telling my mother did not seem like an option. Any talk about sex when I was young marked you as "womanish and fast." We kept all that mess hidden.

I'm writing this to encourage parents to watch everyone around your children. There are some really depraved people in this world. Satan is their father and they are masters of deceit. Watch your girls around big girls as well as boys. When I began remembering this atrocity, I cried because it was so painful. I feel God wanted me to put everything down on paper so I could rid myself of all the mental trash that has rendered my self-esteem way down under the table. This was God's plan for my life. He never said we would have a bed of roses all our lives. Actually, in Psalms 34:19 His Word says, "Many are the afflictions of the righteous, but the Lord delivers him out of them all." So you see, we must "bloom where we are planted," and God will take care of the rest.

Let me also mention another person who really helped me in my younger years to cope with having a troubled marriage. Mrs. Whitman (I don't recall her first name) was my next door neighbor for many years in East Dallas on Frank Street. She was so kind to me. She often talked to me about life and encouraged me to stay with my husband in spite of his wandering ways. She would also keep my children when I had to work. At that time, I worked at Golden Acres, a rest home for Jewish aged on Centerville Road. So sometimes I had to work the weekends. Jay loved to be with his drinking buddies on weekends, so he very often disappeared, and I had no one to keep my children. Many a Sunday, Mrs. Whitman would miss church to keep my kids for me. I only had Ray, Jackie and Jeff at the time. But she was so kind. She told me if I just hung in there with my husband, someday I would be glad I did. That time has come, and I want to say "thank you" to Mrs. Whitman for helping a young wife a mother through some very hard times. I had no family in Dallas, so it was good to have a next-door neighbor who really cared and showed it by her actions.

Through the trying times of raising children, losing children, losing parents, and other really traumatic experiences, God has raised my faith to another level. I now know God is able to do exceedingly, abundantly, above all we can ask or think. I now know he really is a husband for you, when yours is no longer around. There have been times when I was so lonely for my husband and needed him sexually. I cried out to God, "Father, you see how I'm hurting, please help me. He would put me to sleep and calm my spirits. When I awake in the morning, it's like a new beginning (Those new mercies kicking in. Lamentations 3: 22, 23) I have learned He is a friend that sticks closer than a brother, and a husband for women who have no husband or in my case, or a husband for those whose husbands are no longer able to be husbands to them.

Sometimes I cry out, "Lord, how could you allow such and such to happen to me." I tithe my income, I give my time, I I I..... But then the Holy Spirit will say to me, "Are you quite finished with your little pity party? Now sit still and listen to me. You are no better than anyone else. I have mercy on whom I will have mercy. I told you in my Word I will never leave you or forsake you, so, you must be reminded I keep my Word. I love you, and I know what is best for you. When the Lord reprimands you, you really know it. I thank God for the times He chastises me. I know I belong to Him and He'll never put more on me than I can bear.

Before I close, I want to say a few words about "One Body in Christ," a prayer group started by Ms. Magdalene Anderson. I joined about four years ago. It is really a special group. We are an interracial group that gets together once per month for prayer, singing, testimonies and just plain old fellowship. Our main focus is prayer for the lost around us whether relatives, friends or whoever needs Christ. Right now, we meet in their home. Rev. Carl Anderson is her husband. We have some really great, Holy Ghost filled meetings. There is Don and Carol Johnson. Don is our musician and song leader. He plays the keyboard and supplies copies of praise songs, So we can join in and really praise God with our music. Don and Carol have been blessed to go on several missionary trips. They are always so enthusiastic.

There is John, Janet and CC, their little girl. Talk about encouraging! If you are down around John and Janet, you won't be that way long. He will pray for you and remind you of God's promises and Janet will quietly let you know how God has blessed them. There is no way anyone can stay down in the dumps around them. CC is such a sweet girl. She is growing up to be a kind and considerate person. Magdalene and Bro. Carl are the sweetest couple. They maintain our group, so we can continue to meet and flourish. Magdalene or (Mary) as we call her, is so Spirit-filled sometimes it seems to be a house full when there are only four or five of us. I miss Ola Redmond when she cannot come. She is a very special person and part of our group. Also, my good friend, Oretha Johnson who always has a Scripture to encourage us when we are having problems. Sister Rose is so joyful when she is able to be with us. We miss her when she can't be there. We are a loving people, and may God keep One Body in Christ going and going and going in the power of the Holy· Spirit.

As I close my writings, I want to say it is my sincere desire that my children will all come into their spiritual heritage. I brought them up in the nurture and admonition of the Lord. The Bible says in Proverbs 22:6 "Train up a child in the way he should go, and when he is old, he will not depart from it." I believe that with all my heart. Loving God and serving him are the two most important things in our lives. Many people go through an entire lifetime without realizing that fact. God has a plan for all our lives, and it is up to us to recognize that fact and act accordingly.

The title of my book is "Faithful is He", taken from the Scripture I Thess. 5:24 "Faithful is He that calleth you, who also will do it." He has called me out as His child and He has been and will continue to be faithful in His care for me and all of us. As I look back on the many hurts and heartaches, joys and triumphs, He has brought me though. All I can say is Hallelujah, Praise His wonderful Name.

Thank you for reading and for your Support

-Birdie L. Houston-

Faithful is HE

FAMILY TREE INFORMATION

FOR THE BENEFIT OF ALL MY CHILDREN AND GRANDCHILDREN, I AM INCLUDING THE FOLLOWING INFORMATION.

MY MOTHER'S NAME WAS QUINTELLA MARY SMITH

AND MY FATHER'S NAME WAS ALBERT AUSTIN

QUINTELLA WAS BORN 10/18/04 In Noblelake, Arkansas. She died March 7, 1992 in Dallas

Her father's name was: **Johnny Anderson**

Her mother's name was: **Emma Bradley**

Her grandfather's name was: **Billy Anderson**

Billy was of German descent. Mother said He had White skin and made sauerkraut In large wash pots often.

ALBERT WAS BORN 8/04 AND DIED IN OCTOBER, 1958 IN WINK, TEXAS

His mother's name was: **Lizzie**

His father's name was: **Spencer**

His Grandmother's name was: **Maggie Jackson**

His grandfather's name was: **Wash Jackson**

He has a living brother - **L.D. Austin** who lives in Houston, Texas He is now about 87 years old

Jimmie Jay's mother's name was Vinie Taylor Houston and his real father's name was J.D. Grant. He was raised by Charlie Houston, Sr., and carried his name.

ABOUT THE AUTHOR

Birdie Houston was born August 1, 1932 to Quintella and Albert in Wink, Texas. She attended school in Wink, Texas until she was in the 11th grade. At the age of 17, she went to Crockett, Texas and finished high school on the campus of Mary Allen College. They had a high school department there. She then went on to attend college there. Birdie did not complete her college work due to difficulties which came because of irregularities in the administration of grades and finances during her senior year. She was able to complete a years' course in Business Administration at Rutherford's College of Business in 1972. This course enabled her to become employed by the Dallas Public Schools for 21 years. She spent 10 years as senior high school secretary at Lincoln High School, and 11 years at Health Special High School. Birdie is married to Jimmie Jay Houston and they have five children: Jimmy Ray, Jacque' Jaye, Albert Jeffrey, Kimberly Michelle, and Tracy Laverne. They have 13 grandchildren: Carla Nikol, Steven DeJuan, Burshea, Nytosha Yvette, Phillip Michael, Shantell Yvonne, Shayla Kamyra, Jarrell NyQualen, Damonte' Jovan, Karl, Jr., DeAndre' Renard, Alexander Jeffery, and Jimmie Jay, II.; and 5 great-grandchildren: Nyteara, Little Stevie, Zekia, Little Phillip, and Derrick, Jr. She is a member of These Are They Community Church, Rev. Willie J. Bolden is her pastor. She works with the Missions Program, sings in the choir, works with the Deaconess Board and the Building Committee. She had a burning desire to write a book about her life to show how God brought her through the rough times she experienced in growing up in the little West Texas town of Wink, Texas. It has taken five years to complete this book. May the Lord's Name be glorified by those who read it.

Jimmy Ray Houston April 14, 1955

Jacquelyn (Jacque') Jaye Houston Lacy April 2, 1956

Albert Jeffrey Houston April 18, 1958

Kimberly Michelle Houston Johnson November 12, 1961

Tracy Lavern Houston Wynne September 23, 1962

Birdie Houston

Our Family Tree New Additions

Father's Name	Mother's Name	Child's Name	Birth Date

Faithful is HE
Our Family Tree New Additions

Father's Name	Mother's Name	Child's Name	Birth Date

Faithful is HE
In Memoriam

Jimmie Jay Houston I

October 7, 1928 - November 26, 2001

Karl Wayne Wynne

November 12, 1984

- October 29, 2017

We Love You

Always

www.ingramcontent.com/pod-product-compliance
Lightning Source LLC
Chambersburg PA
CBHW031204090426
42736CB00009B/777